The Effortless Dysphagia Diet Cookbook

Easy-to-Follow Minced and Moist
Dysphagia-Friendly Recipes for Safe
Swallowing and Thyroid Function Support

Byron Wood, DCN

COPYRIGHT PAGE

Text Copyright © 2025 Byron Wood, DCN

All Rights Reserved Worldwide

No part of this book may be reproduced, scanned, or distributed in any printed or electronic form without permission. Please do not participate in or encourage piracy of copyrighted materials in violation of the author's rights. Purchase only authorized editions.

This cookbook contains recipes and nutritional insights developed by Byron Wood, DCN. The content is provided for general knowledge and informational purposes. It is not intended as, and shall not be understood or construed as, professional medical or nutritional advice, diagnosis, or treatment. Always seek the advice of your physician or another qualified health provider with any questions you may have regarding a medical condition or dietary needs. Never disregard professional medical advice or delay in seeking it because of something you have read in this book.

TABLE OF CONTENTS

COPYRIGHT PAGE 2

TABLE OF CONTENTS 3

EATING MADE EASY –DYSPHAGIA & SAFE SWALLOWING 1

    Types of Dysphagia 2

    Causes of Dysphagia? 3

    IDDSI Levels and Food Textures Explained 7

    Tips for Enhancing Flavor without Risk 13

BREAKFASTS RECIPES THAT GOES DOWN EASY 19

    Creamy Apple Cinnamon Oatmeal 19

    Mashed Sweet Potatoes with Greek Yogurt 20

    Cornmeal Mush 22

    Cheesy Grits Casserole 22

    Pancake Casserole 24

    Cream of Wheat with Banana-Mango Puree 25

Easy To Chew Oatmeal 26

King of the Morning Muffins 27

Cream of Wheat with Apple Jam 28

Biscuits and Gravy 30

Apple Pie Oatmeal 32

Nutella & Banana Oatmeal 33

Pumpkin Spice Rice Pudding 34

EASY-TO-SWALLOW LUNCH RECIPES 35

Salt Dome Baked Fish 35

Instant Pot Corned Beef and Cabbage Soup 36

(St. Patrick's Day Soup) 36

Split Pea Soup 38

Butternut Squash Soup 39

Zucchini Bisque 40

Carrot and Ginger Soup 41

Tuna Salad with Ritz Crackers 43

Turkey and Wild Rice Soup 44

Soft Cabbage and Noodle Delight 45

Brazilian Beans and Rice 47

Loose Meat Sandwich (Sloppy Joes) 49

Italian Soup 51

Oven Baked Trout 53

Buffalo Chicken Meatloaf 54

Egg Salad and Avocado 55

WARM, WHOLESOME DINNER RECIPES 57

Jalapeño Hummus 57

Heart Attack Chicken 58

Loaded Smashed Potatoes 59

Soft and Cheesy Rice Bites 61

Soft & Creamy Fried Rice 63

Potato Pancakes 64

Herb and Garlic Mashed Potatoes 66

Soft Corn Tortilla Casserole 67

Spaghetti Spaghetti Squash 69

Summer Squash Puree 70

Pink Fluff 71

Glazed Carrots 72

Egg Salad and Avocado 73

SMOOTHIES, SHAKES AND PUREED TREAT RECIPES 75

Strawberry Rhubarb Smoothie 75

Strawberry Lemonade Smoothie 76

Summer Smoothie 76

Zucchini Smoothie 77

Almond Milk 78

Chocolate Cherry Banana Smoothie 79

Blueberry Banana Smoothie 80

Almond Pear Milkshake 81

Mango Pear Smoothie 81

Blueberry Peach Smoothie 82

Mango-Raspberry-Pineapple Smoothie 83

The Banana Milkshake 84

Carrot Cake Smoothie Bowl 84

Chapter One
EATING MADE EASY – DYSPHAGIA & SAFE SWALLOWING

Dysphagia is the medical term for difficulty swallowing. When you swallow, many muscles and nerves work together to move food or drink from your mouth to your stomach. When there's an issue with how these parts work, swallowing may feel uncomfortable or slow. You may cough or choke when you try to swallow water, food or even your own saliva (spit).

Most people know what dysphagia feels like. If you've ever eaten too fast and felt like food went down the wrong pipe, or if you've cleared your throat because something felt stuck — you're already familiar with dysphagia. The feeling's unpleasant, and it's usually not anything to worry about.

But dysphagia can be a sign of something serious. It's a common symptom following a stroke. Untreated dysphagia can pose risks like food or liquid getting into your airway (aspiration). This can lead to a lung infection or pneumonia.

A specialist in swallowing disorders called a speech-language pathologist (SLP) can assess your ability to swallow and provide treatment if there's a risk.

Types of Dysphagia

Healthcare providers separate dysphagia into three types based on where the problem is. Think of swallowing as a journey that foods and liquids take to your stomach. There are three main stops along the way: your mouth (oral cavity), throat (pharynx) and the food tube that connects to your stomach (esophagus).

Issues at any of these key stops can create slowdowns, making it difficult or impossible to swallow.

Oral dysphagia: The problem is in your mouth. Your jaw, teeth and tongue work together to tear food into smaller pieces when you chew. Your salivary glands produce spit that softens the food so it breaks apart easily.

Oropharyngeal dysphagia: The problem is in your throat. After your mouth prepares the food, your tongue pushes it to the back of your throat. Your voice box (larynx) closes to prevent food or liquid from slipping into your airway (trachea) on its way to your esophagus. Oropharyngeal dysphagia is also known as transfer dysphagia. Think of it this way: it involves problems transferring food from your mouth to your throat.

Esophageal dysphagia: The problem is in your esophagus. Your esophagus squeezes the food or liquid down in a wave-like motion (peristalsis) until it reaches your stomach.

Causes of Dysphagia?

Any disorder, disease or condition that impacts the muscles or nerves that help you swallow can cause dysphagia.

Nervous System and Brain Disorders

Conditions and injuries affecting your brain and nervous system (the network of nerves that controls muscles and organs) that cause dysphagia include:

Amyotrophic lateral sclerosis (ALS): A condition that weakens the nerves that control your muscles.

Brain tumors: Growths in your brain (both cancerous and benign) that can disrupt the nerve signals that tell your muscles to move.

Cerebral palsy: A developmental disorder (one you're born with) that makes it hard to move and coordinate muscles.

Dementia: A mental state associated with different diseases that involve trouble thinking and coordinating movement.

Multiple sclerosis (MS): An autoimmune disease that damages the nerves in your brain and spinal cord. With an autoimmune disease, your immune system attacks your body's healthy cells.

Parkinson's disease: A condition that causes tissue in your brain to deteriorate, creating problems with movement and coordination.

Muscle Disorders

Conditions that prevent the muscles in your head and neck from helping you swallow include:

Achalasia: A rare disorder where muscles at the bottom of your esophagus don't relax to allow food to enter your stomach.

Cricopharyngeal spasms: Spasms (abnormal contractions) that happen when the muscle at the top of your esophagus squeezes too much, creating the sensation that something's stuck in your throat. Esophageal spasms. Spasms that happen when various muscles in your esophagus squeeze too much.

Muscular dystrophy: A group of inherited conditions that cause muscles to weaken over time.

Myasthenia gravis: An autoimmune disease that interrupts the signals nerves send to muscles, making it hard to control movements.

Myositis: An autoimmune disease that can cause muscle weakness in your throat and esophagus.

Scleroderma: An autoimmune disease that causes scar tissue to form in your esophagus. The stiff tissue prevents your esophagus muscles from squeezing to move food toward your stomach.

Narrowing, Blockages and Structural Issues

Conditions that create blockages or cause your throat or esophagus to be too narrow can make it hard to swallow. Causes include:

Cancer: Tumors in your head and neck can obstruct food and drink. Esophageal cancer is the most common type of cancer that causes dysphagia.

Eosinophilic esophagitis: A condition that happens when too many white blood cells (eosinophils) build up in your esophagus, causing stiffness.

Esophageal diverticulum: A weakened pouch that forms in the lining of your esophagus. Food bits can collect in the pouch, creating the sensation that something's stuck in your throat. The most common type is called Zenker's diverticulum.

Esophageal webs and (Schatzki) rings: Atypical tissue inside your esophagus that narrows the tube. The smaller tube can cause food to get stuck.

GERD (acid reflux disease): Stomach acid can flow backward into your esophagus, causing scar tissue. The tissue can cause tightening called esophageal strictures and irritation called Barrett's esophagus. These conditions can make swallowing painful and difficult.

Other causes

Infections, like strep throat (bacterial tonsillitis), can cause pain and inflammation that lead to dysphagia. Dysphagia can occur after surgery to your head and neck or other types of treatment. For example, radiation therapy for head and neck cancer destroys tumors but can also damage tissue involved in swallowing.

IDDSI Levels and Food Textures Explained

Level 7 – Regular

What is a Regular diet? It is a diet which:

- Normal, everyday foods of various textures that are developmentally and age
- Any method may be used to eat the foods
- May be hard and crunchy or naturally soft
- Sample size not restricted
- Includes hard, tough, chewy, fibrous, stringy, dry, crispy, crunchy or crumbly bits

- Includes food that contains pips, seeds, pith inside skin, husks or bones
- Includes 'dual consistency' or 'mixed consistency' foods and liquids

Level 7* – Regular Easy Chew

What is Easy chew food?

- Normal, everyday foods of soft/tender texture
- Any method may be used to eat these foods (e.g. fingers, fork, spoon, chopsticks etc.)
- Food piece size is not restricted in size. They can be smaller or bigger than 1.5cm x 1.5cm
- Do not use foods that are: hard, tough, chewy, fibrous, have stringy textures, pip/seeds, bones or gristle
- You should be able to 'bite off' pieces of soft and tender food, so they are safe to swallow without tiring easily
- You should be able to remove bone, gristle or other hard pieces that cannot be swallowed safely from your mouth without help or direction from others.

Level 6 – Soft and Bite-sized

What is a Soft & Bite-sized diet? It is a diet which:

- Can be eaten with a fork, spoon or chopsticks
- Can be mashed/brown down with pressure from fork/spoon/chopsticks
- A knife is not required to cut food, but may be used to help load fork/spoon
- Chewing is required before swallowing
- Is soft, tender, moist throughout
- Has no separate thin liquid
- Bite-sized pieces as appropriate for size and oral processing skills (Paediatric = 8mm pieces, Adults = 15mm pieces)

Testing Method:

1. If you are unsure whether your food is the correct consistency for a Soft and Bite-sized Diet, you can test it using the fork pressure test:
2. Pressure from fork held on its side can be used to cut/break this texture
3. Sample size (1.5×1.5cm) squashes and changes shape (not returning to its original shape) when pressure applied with base of fork (firm pressure – thumb nail blanches to white)

Level 5 – Minced and Moist

- What is a Minced and Moist diet? It is a diet which:
- Can be eaten with a fork or spoon

- Can be scooped and shaped on a plate
- Soft and moist with no separate thin liquid
- Small lumps visible within food (Paediatric= 2mm lump size, Adult = 4mm lump size)
- Lumps are easy to squash with tongue

Testing Method:

1. If you are unsure whether your food is the correct consistency for a Minced & Moist Diet, you can test it using the Fork pressure test:
2. Particles should easily be separated between and come through the prongs of a fork when pressed
3. Particles can be easily mashed with little pressure from a fork
4. This consistency can also be tested using the fork drip test:
5. The scooped sample sits in a pile or can mound on the fork
6. It does not easily or completely flow or fall through the prongs of a fork

N.B. Lump sizes must be no bigger than:

2mm for children

4mm for adults

Level 4 – Pureed

What is a Pureed diet? It is a diet which:

- Is usually eaten with a spoon (fork is possible)
- Does not require chewing
- Can be piped, layered or moulded
- Has no lumps
- Is not sticky
- Liquid must not separate from solid
- Testing Method:
- If you are unsure whether your food is the correct consistency for a Pureed Diet, you can test it using the spoon tilt test:
- Take a spoonful of food and tip it off of the spoon. The food should be:
- cohesive enough to hold its shape on the spoon
- the full spoonful must plop off spoon if tilted/turned sideways (sliding off easily with very little left on the spoon)
- Take a forkful of food. The food should:
- Sit in a mound or pile above the fork
- A small amount may flow through and fork a tail below the fork
- Does not dollop, flow or drip continuously through the fork prongs

Level 3 – Liquidised

What is a liquidised diet? It is a diet which:

- Cannot be piped, layered or moulded on a plate
- Cannot be eaten with a fork because it drips slowly in dollops through the prongs
- Can be eaten with a spoon
- No oral processing/chewing required—can be swallowed directly
- Smooth texture with no 'bits' (lumps, fibres, bits of shell or skins, husk, particles of gristle or bone)
- Testing Method:
- If you are unsure whether your food is the correct consistency for a Liquidised Diet, you can test it using the fork drip test:
- Scoop up the food with a fork
- The food should drip slowly or in dollops/strands through the slots of the fork

Transitional Foods

What are Transitional Foods? They are foods which:

- start as one texture (e.g. firm solid) and change into another texture specifically when moisture (e.g. water or saliva) is applied, or when a change in temperature occurs (e.g. heating)

Testing Method:

1. If you are unsure whether your food is a transitional food, you can test it using the fork pressure test:
2. After moisture or temperature has been applied, the sample can be easily deformed and does not recover its shape when force is lifted

Tips for Enhancing Flavor without Risk

1. Do not advance prep onions and garlic

This is best done last minute as the odors and flavors of onion and garlic intensify over time. Macerating onions for a salad in a little red wine vinegar tames their pungency and softens the texture.

2. Out those sprouts

Remove any green shoots from garlic cloves before chopping or cooking them. Their bitter compounds persist even after cooking.

3. Keep the taste in Tomatoes

Buy only as many tomatoes as you can easily store and use. Tomatoes are not meant for the refrigerator – the cold will destroy the flavor compounds of tomatoes, so be sure to keep them on the bench top or table.

For tasty tomato salads -resist recipe Directions to deseed tomatoes. The jellied insides is where most of the flavor is bound. In fact the guts of the tomatoes contains three times the amount of flavor enhancing glutamic acid than the flesh.

4. Unpack your Meat and Chicken packages as soon as you get them home

Remove all the plastic wrappings and leave the meat uncovered in the refrigerator. Dehydrating the outside of the flesh and patting it completely dry before cooking, will enable the meat to brown and crisp up more easily.

5. Salt meats before cooking.

Penetration of the salt into the flesh is a type of dry brining. The salt brings out all of the natural flavors of the meat. Surprise yourself! Salt steaks and chops 2– 24 hours before cooking, larger pieces of meat on the bone should be salted up to 2 days before cooking.

Salt a whole chicken up to 24 hours in advance. Use kosher salt and be liberal in its application. It is less salty than table salt and its larger grains cling better to the meat's surface. If you cannot use the salted meat, just wrap and freeze it -label it as salted and thaw it out in the refrigerator when you are ready to use it.

6. Always bring meat to room temperature before cooking.

This enables more even cooking of the meat. Remove the meat from the fridge 30 minutes to 2 hours before cooking it for best results. Raw meat should not be left unrefrigerated for any more than 2 hours.

7. Cooking

8. Always gently preheat your pots and pans before adding any Ingredients

Do this just for a few minutes, over a gentle heat to facilitate even cooking and to minimize the pan losing too much heat as **Ingredients** get added. This loss of heat slows down the browning process

9. Buy yourself a heat diffuser mat

They sit over gas flames or on ceramic cook tops. They are brilliant for evenly distributing the heat in cookware that doesnt have a very thick base. It reduces the impact of hot spots on cookware. When you have trouble getting a very low simmer – place this mat over your lowest flame and it will reduce the impact of the heat significantly.

10. Sprinkle a little sugar on top

Lightly sprinkling lean proteins and even vegetables with the tiniest pinch of sugar, helps them brown better and faster, enhancing flavor without over cooking.

11. Add a rind to soups and stews

Save your parmesan cheese rinds. Store them in snap lock bags in the freezer for an indefinite time. Don't worry to thaw them, simply add them to simmering tomato based soups and stews for extra savory depth of flavor.

12. Don't forget to scrape the pan

I am not talking about bitter, crumbly, charred remains but the caramelized brown bits stuck to the bottom of the pan. These are easily removed and add extra savory flavor to sauces, soups and stews. Simply add only a few tablespoons of water, wine or broth to the pan and gently nudge the browned bits from the base, using a wooden spoon. Continue cooking them over low heat until they are incorporated into the liquid. Strain before using if you like.

13. Flip or stir meat while marinating

Marinating is not entirely set and forget. If you seal the meat and the marinade in a snap lock bag, and rest it in a container in the fridge, it is easy to pick it up and flip it over, making sure that all of the meat is covered with the marinade. Alternatively arrange the ingredients in a covered baking dish. Half way through marinating uncover, turn the meat – coating all surfaces with the marinade. Cover and return to the refrigerator.

14. Trim beef stew meat thoroughly; leave a little fat on the pork

Ask the butcher to be sure to remove the hard fat and connective tissue from the exterior of the beef before cooking. The intramuscular marbling will provide the flavoring and tenderizing that you need. With pork however, reserve a thin layer (about .5cm) of fat on the meat for extra flavor. It is worth asking the butcher too for a pig's trotter or some pork skin to add to your beef and pork stews. This makes the sauce especially silky.

15. Keep fat fresh tasting

Fat is one of the most important flavor agents in cooking. The fats though in fatty acids, butters, oils and oil rich **Ingredients** like nuts are prone to rancidity. This is because they easily absorb other flavors and they are ill affected by light and heat. Best storage methods:

2 Chapter Two
BREAKFASTS RECIPES THAT GOES DOWN EASY

Creamy Apple Cinnamon Oatmeal

Ingredients

Oatmeal

- ½ cup old fashioned rolled oats
- 1 cup water or milk
- ½ Tablespoon maple syrup, brown sugar or coconut sugar (optional)
- ¼-½ teaspoon ground cinnamon
- ½ teaspoon vanilla extract
- pinch of sea salt
- 2 Tablespoons chopped pecans, for topping

Cinnamon Apples

- ½ cup diced apples

- 2 teaspoons maple syrup
- ¼ teaspoon cinnamon

Directions

1. In a small saucepan combine diced apples, maple syrup and cinnamon and saute for a few minutes until apples are soft and look similar to baked apples. Set aside.
2. Add oats, water, maple syrup, cinnamon, vanilla and salt to a saucepan over medium-high heat. Bring mixture to a low boil, reduce heat to a low simmer and continue to cook for about 5-7 minutes; stirring occasionally. Oatmeal is ready when the oats have soaked up most of the liquid and are creamy.
3. Transfer to a bowl and top with cinnamon apples, pecans, and a sprinkle of cinnamon and additional sweetener if needed.

Nutrition Facts (per serving)

Calories 320 | Fat 12g | Carbohydrates 50g | Protein 5g

Mashed Sweet Potatoes with Greek Yogurt

Ingredients

- 2 pounds sweet potatoes or yams, peeled and cut into 1/2 inch pieces
- 1 tablespoon brown sugar
- 1 tablespoon maple syrup
- 1/2 teaspoon ground cinnamon
- 1/2 cup Greek yogurt

Directions

1. Place the sweet potatoes in a large pot and fill with cold water to cover the potatoes. Bring the water to a boil over high heat, then reduce heat to medium-low and then simmer for 10-15 minutes or until the sweet potatoes are tender when pierced with a fork.
2. Drain the sweet potatoes in a colander, shaking the colander to help remove excess water. Pour the potatoes into a large bowl.
3. Add the brown sugar, maple syrup, cinnamon, and Greek yogurt to the sweet potatoes. Mash to your desired texture and serve warm.

Nutrition Facts (per serving)

Calories 220 | Fat 2g | Carbohydrates 45g | Protein 5g

Cornmeal Mush

Ingredients

- 1 cup yellow cornmeal
- 2 cups water
- 1 pinch salt
- 2 tablespoons heavy cream
- 2 tablespoons white sugar

Directions

1. Mix the cornmeal, water, and salt together in a small saucepan. Cook on medium heat for about 3-5 minutes, until the mixture is thick.
2. Top with heavy cream and sugar before serving.

Nutrition Facts (per serving)

Calories 200 | Fat 8g | Carbohydrates 30g | Protein 2g

Cheesy Grits Casserole

Ingredients

- 2¼ cups water
- 2¼ cups milk

- 1 teaspoon salt
- 1 cup quick grits
- 8 ounces shredded cheddar cheese
- ¼ cup butter
- ⅛ teaspoon garlic powder
- 1 cup diced ham (to make the ham easier to chew, you can run it through a food processor)
- 2 eggs

Directions

1. In a large saucepan on medium/high heat, bring the water, milk, and salt to a boil. Stir in the quick grits. Cook for 5-6 minutes (while stirring) until it thickens.
2. Stir in the cheese, butter, and garlic powder. Once the cheese and butter are melted, stir in the ham. Let the grits cool down enough that you can put your finger in it without getting burned. You can put it in the fridge to speed the cooling up.
3. Once the grits have cooled down, mix in the eggs.
4. Pour the finished mixture into a 9x13 pan which has been sprayed with cooking spray. Bake in the oven for 45 minutes at 350°F.
5. Top with shredded cheese and green onions if you'd like!

Nutrition Facts (per serving)

Calories 360 | Fat 20g | Carbohydrates 30g | Protein 15g

Pancake Casserole

Ingredients

- 1¼ cups buttermilk (see "food for thought" section for buttermilk substitute)
- 1 egg
- 3 tablespoons melted butter
- 1½ cups flour (I use half white flour and half wheat flour)
- 1 tablespoon sugar
- 1½ teaspoons baking powder
- ½ teaspoon baking soda
- ¼ teaspoon salt
- extra sugar to top the batter before baking
- Your choice of pancake casserole filling (you can add fruit, berries, even chocolate chips to the top of the batter before baking)

Directions

1. In a mixing bowl, combine buttermilk, eggs, and the melted butter. Then add the flour, sugar, baking powder, baking soda, and salt. Stir until combined.

2. Line a 9x13 glass pan with parchment paper and spray with cooking spray. Evenly spread the batter in the pan. Sprinkle any desired **Ingredients** (fruit or chocolate chips) on top of the batter before baking.
3. Bake at 400°F for 15 minutes. When a knife is inserted in and comes out clean, it's done. Top with anything you like: fruit, whipped cream, maple syrup, etc.

Nutrition Facts (per serving)

Calories 280 | Fat 12g | Carbohydrates 35g | Protein 6g

Cream of Wheat with Banana-Mango Puree

Ingredients

- 2 servings cooked Cream of Wheat
- 1 cup frozen mango
- ½ banana
- 1 teaspoon lime juice
- 1 tablespoon honey

Directions

1. Cook the cream of wheat as directed on the package.

2. To make the puree, add the mango, banana, lime juice, and honey to a blender and blend on high until smooth. Add the puree to the cooked cream of wheat. Don't be shy, pour it on like ice cream over a hot brownie.

Nutrition Facts (per serving)

Calories 250 | Fat 2g | Carbohydrates 55g | Protein 4g

Easy To Chew Oatmeal

Ingredients

- 2 cups rolled oats
- 4 cups water

Directions

1. Add the rolled oats to a blender. Blend on high until it is the same consistency as baking flour.
2. In a medium pot, bring the water to a boil. Slowly add the oat flour to the boiling water while stirring (this keeps it from clumping). Stir until thickened (which doesn't take long, it cooks almost instantly).
3. Top with anything you want, my favorite is to simply top with brown sugar. If you want the oatmeal to be a thinner consistency, just use more water than directed.

Nutrition Facts (per serving)

Calories 150 | Fat 2g | Carbohydrates 30g | Protein 5g

King of the Morning Muffins

Ingredients

- 1 cup Bob's Red Mill 10 Grain Hot Cereal (run it through a blender if you want the muffin texture to be fine, otherwise it will be coarse but still very chewable)
- 1¼ cup buttermilk
- ½ cup white sugar
- ⅓ cup softened butter
- 1 egg
- 1 cup flour
- 1 teaspoon salt
- 1 teaspoon baking powder
- 1 teaspoon baking soda
- the zest of one orange
- ¼ cup white sugar

Directions

1. Mix the cereal and buttermilk in a small bowl and let it rest for 10 minutes.
2. In a large bowl, beat the butter and the 1/2 cup of sugar together, then mix in the egg.
3. Add the cereal/buttermilk mix, the remaining dry ingredients, and half the orange zest, stir until mixed.
4. Take the other half of orange zest and mix it with 1/4 cup of sugar.
5. Line a muffin pan with cupcake liners. Spoon the batter into the cupcake liners, filling each between 1/2-3/4 full. Sprinkle each muffin with the zest/sugar mix.
6. Bake at 400° F for 15 minutes.

Nutrition Facts (per serving)

Calories 340 | Fat 16g | Carbohydrates 45g | Protein 6g

Cream of Wheat with Apple Jam

Ingredients

- 2 pounds apples chopped in ½ inch pieces (any kind of apple will work)
- 1½ cup water
- 1 cup sugar
- 2 tablespoons lemon juice

- 1 cinnamon stick
- cooked cream of wheat

Directions

1. In a sauce pan on high heat, combine water and chopped apples and bring water to a boil. Cook for about 15 minutes, apples will start to become soft
2. Add sugar and reduce heat to medium. While stirring frequently, cook for another 25 minutes, mixture will start becoming more jam like.
3. Stir in the lemon juice and the cinnamon stick. Reduce heat to a simmer and cook for 5 more minutes. Turn of the heat and let it rest for 5 minutes. The jam should be thicker at this point, if you would like it thicker then no worries, just cook it longer. Take out the cinnamon stick and store in the fridge.
4. When you are ready for breakfast, cook your desired amount of cream of wheat (as directed on packaging) and stir however much apple jam you want.

Nutrition Facts (per serving)

Calories 290 | Fat 1g | Carbohydrates 70g | Protein 2g

Biscuits and Gravy

Ingredients

Biscuit Ingredients

- 2 cups flour
- 1 tablespoon baking powder
- ½ teaspoon salt
- ¼ cup shortening
- ¼ cup butter
- ¾ cup milk

Gravy Ingredients

- 1 pound breakfast sausage
- ⅓ cup flour
- 4 cups milk
- salt and pepper to taste

Directions

Biscuit Directions

1. Get your oven preheating to 450° F. In a large bowl, mix the flour, baking powder, and salt. Chop up the shortening and butter into 1/4 inch cubes and add to

the four mixture, use two forks to further break the shortening down until the mixture turns into crumbs.
2. Add the milk to the mixture while stirring, keep stirring until it forms a soft/sticky dough.
3. Put the dough on a lightly floured surface and roll it out, it will become less sticky as your roll it. Roll it into a 1/2 inch thick sheet and use your most trusted cookie cutter to cut out your biscuits. Place the biscuits on a cookie sheet lined with parchment paper, bake for about 10 minutes, until biscuits are a golden brown.

Gravy Directions

1. In a pan or a skillet, break up the sausage into small pieces. On medium-high heat, cook the sausage until browned all the way through. Reduce the heat to medium-low. Add half of the flour, let the sausage soak it up, then sprinkle the rest of the flour, little by little, and stir it for about a minute. Add the milk while stirring constantly.
2. Continue to cook until the gravy thickens (It can take a while, like 10-ish minutes) Add salt and pepper to taste.
3. Top Biscuits with the gravy and serve while hot!

Nutrition Facts (per serving)

Calories 520 | Fat 32g | Carbohydrates 40g | Protein 15g

Apple Pie Oatmeal

Ingredients

- 2 cups cooked oatmeal
- 1 diced apple (any apple will work, use your favorite)
- 2 tablespoons butter
- ½ teaspoon cinnamon
- ¼ cup water
- 1 tablespoon brown sugar
- caramel sauce as a topping

Directions

1. Use a saucepan on a stove set to medium heat and melt the butter. Add the diced apples, brown sugar, cinnamon, and water and cook for 10-15 minutes, until the apples are soft and the mixture is a jammy consistency
2. Cook oatmeal as directed on packaging. Combine the oatmeal and cooked apples. Top with caramel sauce and eat!

Nutrition Facts (per serving)

Calories 320 | Fat 14g | Carbohydrates 45g | Protein 4g

Nutella & Banana Oatmeal

Ingredients

- 1 cup oats
- 3 tablespooons Nutella
- 1 mashed banana

Directions

1. Cook oats as directed on packaging.
2. Add Nutella and the mashed banana to the cooked oatmeal. Stir until combined.

Nutrition Facts (per serving)

Calories 370 | Fat 16g | Carbohydrates 50g | Protein 6g

Pumpkin Spice Rice Pudding

Ingredients

- ½ cup cooked rice
- ½ cup pumpkin puree
- ½ cup milk
- ½ teaspoon cinnamon
- 1 teaspoon maple syrup

Directions

1. In a saucepan, combine cooked rice, pumpkin puree, milk, cinnamon, and maple syrup.

2. Heat gently over low heat until warm and creamy.

3. Serve warm or chilled.

Nutrition Facts (per serving)

Calories 180 | Fat 3g | Carbohydrates 35g | Protein 3g

3   Chapter Three
EASY-TO-SWALLOW LUNCH RECIPES

Salt Dome Baked Fish

Ingredients

- 3 pounds kosher salt
- 4 egg whites
- 2 pounds Whole Red Snapper (or any other whole fish)
- 2 Lemons (sliced)
- 4-6 sprigs fresh parsley

Directions

1. Set the oven for 450°F. Combine the salt, egg whites, with 1/4 cup of water in a mixing bowl. It will have the consistency of wet sand.
2. Line a cooking sheet with parchment paper. Use about 1/3 of your egg/salt mixture to make a 1/2 inch layer as a base to put the fish on. Make this base layer about the same shape as the fish you are using. Place

your clean and gutted whole fish on the base. Fill the inside cavity of the fish with the parsley and sliced lemons.
3. Coat the fish with the remaining egg/salt mixture. it's okay if the tail sticks out.
4. Bake in the oven for 15-20 minutes, until the fish has an internal temperature of 130°F. Let it rest out of the oven for 10 minutes before serving. Use a spoon to crack open the hardened salt dome and enjoy the perfectly cooked fish found within!

Nutrition Facts (per serving)

Calories 180 | Fat 4g | Carbohydrates 0g | Protein 35g

Instant Pot Corned Beef and Cabbage Soup

(St. Patrick's Day Soup)

Ingredients

- 1 tablespoon olive oil
- 2 chopped leeks (cut the leaves off, just chop up the base)
- 2 cloves minced garlic
- 4 chopped carrots (medium or large carrots)
- 1 chopped red pepper

- 1 ½ pounds corned beef (plus the seasoning that comes with the meat)
- 6 cups water
- 2 bay leaves
- 1 cup chopped potatoes (I like to use the small fancy looking baby potatoes)
- chopped fresh parsley (to garnish soup before serving)
- 6 cups chopped cabbage

Directions

1. Press the "Saute" button on the instant pot and add the olive oil, leeks, carrots, red pepper, and garlic. Cook while stirring for 5 minutes.
2. Add the corned beef with it's seasonings, the bay leaves, and the water. Seal the instant pot and cook at high pressure for 70 minutes. Release the pressure.
3. Remove the cooked corned beef and set it aside. Add the potatoes and cabbage. Seal the instant pot and cook on high pressure for an additional 6 minutes. Release the pressure. Shred and chop the cooked corned beef and add it back to the soup. Garnish with fresh parsley and serve.

Nutrition Facts (per serving)

Calories 400 | Fat 25g | Carbohydrates 25g | Protein 30g

Split Pea Soup

Ingredients

- 6 cups chicken broth
- 16 ounces dried split green peas
- 1 diced onion
- 3 large diced carrots
- ¼ teaspoon pepper
- ½ teaspoon salt
- 1 cup cooked diced ham

Directions

1. Put all ingredients into a large crock pot. Cook on high for 4 hours.
2. Test the peas to make sure they are soft, then transfer in batches to a blender and blend until smooth.

Nutrition Facts (per serving)

Calories 350 | Fat 6g | Carbohydrates 55g | Protein 25g

Butternut Squash Soup

Ingredients

- 3 pounds butternut squash
- 6 cups water
- 1 teaspoon salt
- ½ cup heavy cream
- 1 teaspoon brown sugar
- 1 dash nutmeg
- 1½ teaspoons curry powder optional
- 1/4 cup plain yogurt, 2 tablespoons cilantro, 1 teaspoon lime juice (all mixed together) optional topping

Directions

1. Cut the butternut squash in half and scrape out all the seeds and pulp
2. In a pot, add water and salt and bring to a boil. Reduce the heat to medium low, add the squash with the cut side down in a steamer basket and put it in the pot. Cover and continue to cook for 30 minutes, make sure the squash is tender. Take the squash out and scrape out the flesh with a big spoon, be careful, its hot! Use a strainer to strain the steamed liquid from the pot, keep 2-3 cups of the strained liquid.

3. You are now going to add some of the scraped out squash into a blender and add some of the strained liquid. Do small batches at a time and don't fill the blender more than halfway. Add the squash first and a little liquid, adding a little more while pulsing until you reach the proper smooth soup-like consistency (add the optional curry while blending if you want a fun additional flavor). Pour out the blended soup into a pot. Once all the squash is blended, add the cream, brown sugar, and any extra steamed liquid if you want it thinner. Cook the soup on medium heat for 3-5 minutes. Add the nutmeg. Extra salt can be added to taste. you can top it with the optional mixture of yogurt, cilantro, and lime juice.

Nutrition Facts (per serving)

Calories 180 | Fat 8g | Carbohydrates 25g | Protein 3g

Zucchini Bisque

Ingredients

- 4 cups chopped zucchini
- 2 cups water
- 1 cup tomato juice

- 2 tablespoons minced onion
- 2 teaspoons chicken bullion
- ¼ teaspoon dried basil
- 16 ounces cream cheese (cut into cubes)

Directions

1. In a medium or large saucepan, add the zucchini, water, tomato juice, onion, chicken bullion, and basil. Bring to a boil then simmer for 20 minutes.
2. Add the cooked soup to a blender and add the cream cheese. Blend until desired smoothness is reached (depending on the size of your blender, you may have to blend the soup in several batches). Now it is ready to serve!

Nutrition Facts (per serving)

Calories 220 | Fat 18g | Carbohydrates 10g | Protein 6g

Carrot and Ginger Soup

Ingredients

- 2 tablespoons canola oil
- 1½ pounds carrots (peeled and diced)

- 1 diced onion
- 2 tablespoons grated fresh ginger
- 3 cups chicken broth
- ¾ cup milk
- ¼ cup orange juice
- salt and pepper to taste

Directions

1. In a large sauce pan, heat the oil and cook the carrots and onions for 10 minutes over medium heat
2. Transfer the carrots and onions to a pot, add the grated ginger and cook for less than a minute on medium heat
3. Add the broth and bring to a boil, then reduce to a simmer and and cook, covered, over medium-low heat for 15-20 minutes, until the veggies are very soft.
4. Move the soup to a blender and blend until smooth. Transfer it back into the pot.
5. Stir in the milk and the orange juice, heat it back up. Once the soup is hot, it is ready to serve. Use salt and pepper to season.

Nutrition Facts (per serving)

Calories 140 | Fat 7g | Carbohydrates 18g | Protein 2g

Tuna Salad with Ritz Crackers

Ingredients

- 6 ounces solid white albacore tuna (canned)
- 2 tablespoons mayonnaise
- 1 teaspoon Dijon mustard
- 1 teaspoon lemon juice
- salt and pepper to taste
- Ritz crackers

Directions

1. Open the can of tuna and drain it.
2. It's important that you shred the tuna as finely as you can. I like to take my fork and poke it into an open can of tuna and twist it like I'm twisting spaghetti. Then dump the flaky fish into a bowl.
3. Add all the other ingredients and mix it up. Serve with Ritz crackers

Nutrition Facts (per serving)

Calories 320 | Fat 20g | Carbohydrates 15g | Protein 25g

Turkey and Wild Rice Soup

Ingredients

- 1 tablespoon butter
- 2 tablespoons olive oil
- ½ cup chopped carrots
- 1 cup chopped celery
- ½ cup chopped onion
- ¼ teaspoon dried thyme
- ¼ teaspoon dried rosemary
- 6 cups turkey broth (chicken broth could be used alternatively)
- ¾ cups wild rice (you could use white rice if wild rice is too hard for you to chew)
- 2 teaspoons salt
- ½ teaspoon pepper
- 1 cup milk
- ⅓ cup flour
- 3-4 cups cooked turkey meat (any white or dark leftover turkey meat works great) (cooked chicken could be used alternatively)

Directions

1. In a large pot, cook the carrots, celery, onion, thyme, and rosemary in the butter and oil for 5

minutes on medium heat, be sure to stir it frequently.
2. Add the broth, rice, salt, and pepper. Heat to a simmer and cook while stirring for about 30-40 minutes. The wild rice will start bursting when it is cooked enough.
3. In a small bowl, stir the flour and milk together until it is clump free and smooth. Slowly pour it into the soup while stirring. Continue to simmer while stirring for 5 minutes. This step thickens the soup.
4. Add the cooked turkey and cook for a few more minutes. Once the soup and turkey are hot, it is ready to serve. If you have any troubles with the texture or trouble chewing it, don't be afraid to toss the soup in a blender and break it down further, It will still taste great!

Nutrition Facts (per serving)

Calories 360 | Fat 18g | Carbohydrates 30g | Protein 25g

Soft Cabbage and Noodle Delight

Ingredients

4 cups purple cabbage, finely shredded

2 tablespoons olive oil

1/2 cup onion, finely chopped

1/4 cup apple cider vinegar

1 tablespoon sugar

1/2 cup vegetable broth

2 cups soft egg noodles (well-cooked and chopped into smaller pieces)

Salt and pepper to taste

Directions

Heat olive oil in a large skillet or pot over medium heat. Add the chopped onions and sauté for 3-4 minutes until soft.

Add the shredded cabbage and cook for another 5 minutes, stirring occasionally.

Stir in the apple cider vinegar, sugar, and vegetable broth. Reduce heat and let simmer for 10-15 minutes, or until the cabbage is soft and tender.

Meanwhile, cook the egg noodles in a separate pot, ensuring they are soft and easy to chew. Drain and chop them into smaller pieces if needed.

Add the noodles to the cabbage mixture and stir to combine. Let cook for another 5 minutes to allow the flavors to meld together.

Season with salt and pepper to taste. Serve warm.

Nutrition Facts (per serving)

150 Calories | 7g Fat | 22g Carbs | 3g Protein

Brazilian Beans and Rice

Ingredients

The Beans

- 1 tablespoon olive oil
- ⅔ cup diced onion
- 2 cloves minced garlic
- 2 (15 ounce) cans black beans (drained and rinsed)
- 1 cup chicken broth (you could alternatively use 1 cup of water mixed with 1 teaspoon chicken bullion)

- ¼ teaspoon cumin
- ¼ teaspoon oregano
- ¼ teaspoon coriander
- ½ teaspoon salt
- ¼ teaspoon pepper
- the juice of one lime

The Rice

- 1½ cups long grain white rice
- 3 cups chicken broth (or 3 cups of water mixed with 3 teaspoons of chicken bullion)
- 1 teaspoon salt
- 1 teaspoon sugar
- ¼ cup chopped fresh cilantro
- juice of ½ a lime

Directions

The Rice

1. In a large saucepan, bring the rice and chicken broth to a boil on high heat.
2. Once boiling, reduce heat to low and cover the saucepan. Simmer for 20 minutes.
3. Remove from heat and let rest for 5 minutes.
4. Stir in the lime juice and the cilantro.

The Beans

1. In a big skillet, heat olive oil on medium high heat. Add the onions and cook them for 3 minutes, until they start to turn clear. Add the garlic and cook for 30 seconds.
2. Add the beans, broth, and the seasonings. On low heat, cook for 7-8 minutes while stirring.
3. Remove from heat and add the lime juice. Mash the beans with a spatula until the beans are the consistency you want.
4. Serve the beans with the rice.

Nutrition Facts (per serving)

Calories 450 | Fat 10g | Carbohydrates 70g | Protein 20g

Loose Meat Sandwich (Sloppy Joes)

Ingredients

- 2 tablespoons vegetable oil
- 1 large chopped onion
- 2½ pounds ground beef
- 2 tablespoons tomato paste

- ⅔ cup BBQ sauce (I love Sweet Baby Ray's BBQ Sauce)
- ½ cup ketchup
- ¼ cup Worcestershire Sauce
- ¼ cup soy sauce
- 8-12 soft hamburger buns

Directions

1. Heat the oil in a skillet over medium heat. Add onions and cook until they turn clear, which takes between 3-5 minutes. Add the ground beef and stir while chopping it up with a sturdy spatula. Cook until the beef is thoroughly browned all the way through, this takes about 10 minutes. Drain off the extra fat.
2. Mix in the tomato paste, try to get it to coat all the meat evenly. Then add the BBQ sauce, ketchup, and Worcestershire Sauce. Bring this all to a boil while stirring. In about 4-5 minutes it will start to thicken up a bit.
3. Apply the cooked meat generously to a soft hamburger bun and eat. Let the bun soak up the delicious juices, it will be easier to chew.

Nutrition Facts (per serving)

Calories 420 | Fat 20g | Carbohydrates 43g | Protein 32g

Italian Soup

Ingredients

The Soup

- 1 pound ground beef
- ½ cup chopped onion
- ½ cup chopped carrots
- 2 cloves minced garlic
- 1 (28 oz) can crushed tomatoes
- 1 (14.5 oz) can diced tomatoes
- 1 teaspoon dried basil
- 1 teaspoon dried oregano
- ½ teaspoon salt
- 6 cups chicken broth
- 8-10 ounces mini farfalle pasta

Cheesy Topping

- 1 cup Ricotta cheese
- 1 cup shredded mozzarella cheese
- ½ cup grated Parmesan cheese
- ½ teaspoon dried basil
- 1 pinch salt and pepper

Directions

The Soup

1. In a large pot, add the ground beef, onion, carrots, and garlic and cook on medium-high heat (while stirring), until the meat is browned all the way through and the vegetables are softened. Use a strainer to remove excess grease.
2. Add the tomatoes, basil, oregano, and salt. Stir well to make sure things don't stick to the bottom.
3. Add the chicken broth and continue to stir over medium-high heat until the soup starts to simmer/gentle boil.
4. Now add the mini farfalle pasta, cook, while stirring, for as long as is needed to cook the pasta, as directed on the pasta packaging (my box says 8 minutes). Test the pasta to make sure it is done to your liking.

The Cheesy Topping

1. Combine the ricotta, mozzarella, Parmesan, basil, salt, and pepper and stir together until they are well mixed.
2. Top the finished soup with a generous dollop of the cheesy topping and serve while hot.

Nutrition Facts (per serving)

Calories 580 | Fat 32g | Carbohydrates 26g | Protein 52g

Oven Baked Trout

Ingredients

- 1-2 fresh rainbow trout
- 2-3 tablespoons olive oil
- salt and pepper

Directions

1. Clean and butterfly the rainbow trout. There are some great tutorials online if you need help cleaning and butterflying them.
2. Coat the trout in olive oil and season with salt and pepper.
3. Fold the trout up in an aluminum foil pouch and bake in oven at 400° F for 10-15 minutes, until the internal temperature is at least 145° F.

Nutrition Facts (per serving)

Calories 420 | Fat 22g | Carbohydrates 35g | Protein 25g

Buffalo Chicken Meatloaf

Ingredients

- 1 tablespoon olive oil
- ½ cup diced celery
- 1 diced onion
- 1½ pounds ground chicken
- 1 egg
- 2 tablespoons flour
- 2 tablespoons Frank's Hot Sauce

Directions

1. In a small pan, heat oil and add the celery and onion. Cook until they become soft, about 3-4 minutes.
2. In a mixing bowl, mix in the chicken, egg, flour, hot sauce, and the cooked celery and onion. Once it is well mixed, add to a bread pan sprayed with cooking spray.
3. Bake for 60 minutes at 350° F. Let cool for 10-15 minutes before slicing and eating. I like to top it with more Frank's hot sauce.

Nutrition Facts (per serving)

Calories 280 | Fat 14g | Carbohydrates 10g | Protein 25g

Egg Salad and Avocado

Ingredients

- 2 eggs
- 1 tablespoon mayonnaise
- 1 teaspoon mustard
- 1 ripe avocado

Directions

1. Put eggs in a small pot, cover them with an inch of lukewarm water. Cook on medium heat until it reaches a rolling boil. Immediately turn off the stove and cover the pot. Let it sit for 10 minutes.
2. Drain the water and fill the pot back up with ice cold water, this stops the eggs from cooking.
3. Peel the eggs and dice them. Stir in the mayonnaise and the mustard.
4. Slice the avocado and take out the pit. Fill each half with egg salad and eat with your favorite spoon.

Nutrition Facts (per serving)

Calories 320 | Fat 24g | Carbohydrates 12g | Protein 14g

4 Chapter Four
WARM, WHOLESOME DINNER RECIPES

Jalapeño Hummus

Ingredients

- ½ cup cilantro
- 1-2 jalapenos, seeded (1 or 2 depending on how much spice you like)
- 4 garlic cloves
- 4 tablespoons tahini
- 2 tablespoons olive oil
- 3 tablespoons lemon juice
- ¼ cup water
- 1 (15 ounce) can garbanzo beans
- ⅛ teaspoon cumin
- 1 dash cayenne pepper
- ½ teaspoon salt

Directions

1. Combine all ingredients in a blender or food processor. Pulse until smooth. Add salt to taste. Serve with cooked veggies or naan bread. Heck, eat it plain if you want!

Nutrition Facts (per serving)

Calories 100 | Fat 7g | Carbohydrates 8g | Protein 3g

Heart Attack Chicken

Ingredients

- 1 (10.5 ounce) can cream of mushroom soup
- 1 (10.5 ounce) can cream of chicken soup
- 3 frozen chicken breasts
- 1 tablespoon cornstarch
- 1 tablespoon cold water
- parika to optionally garnish with

Directions

1. Take a crock-pot. Add the chicken. Pour in both cans of the condensed soups. Cook on high for 4 hours or on low for 6-8 hours.

2. When it's done cooking, transfer the chicken to a cutting board and chop into denture bite sized pieces. Or you could take two forks and shred the chicken that way.
3. mix the cold water and cornstarch together and slowly add to the liquid in the crock-pot, stirring while you pour it in. This will make the liquid thicker. Once thickened, add the chicken back into the crock-pot
4. Cook your favorite rice as directed on its packaging. Put a generous amount of the chicken and sauce over rice and top with a dash of paprika.

Nutrition Facts (per serving)

Calories 420 | Fat 26g | Carbohydrates 24g | Protein 30g

Loaded Smashed Potatoes

Ingredients

- 6 small potatoes, or a few more if using mini potatoes

- 1 1/2 Tablespoon vegetable or canola oil, DIVIDED

- 1 teaspoon Kosher salt

- 4 slices bacon, cooked and crumbled

- 1 1/2 cups shredded cheddar cheese

- 1 Tablespoon butter

- Salt and Pepper

- Sour Cream, for garnish

- Sliced green onions, for garnish

Directions

1. Wash your potatoes, if necessary, and poke a few times with a knife. Place on to a microwave safe plate and microwave until mostly cooked, about 10 minutes. (You can also boil them to this point, if you prefer. Allow to dry before placing in skillet).

2. Preheat oven to 425°F (regular bake setting/not fan assisted) Place 1 Tbsp. oil in bottom of skillet and brush a bit up the side. Sprinkle the bottom of the pan with 1 tsp. of kosher salt. Place pre-cooked potatoes in to skillet and place in the oven for about 10 minutes, or until very tender. Remove skillet from oven and, using a potato masher, smash each of the potatoes, until quite thin. Place a small pat of butter on top of each potato and season with salt and pepper. Brush the outside of the potatoes with the remaining 1/2 Tbsp. of oil. Return to the oven for another 5-10 minutes or so, or until they crisp up. Remove from

oven again and top with crumbled bacon and shredded cheese. Return to the oven until the cheese is melted and bubbly.

3. Garnish with dollops of sour cream and sliced green onion.

Nutrition Facts (per serving)

Calories 221 | Protein 8g | Fat: 20g

Soft and Cheesy Rice Bites

Ingredients

2 cups cooked creamy risotto (made with vegetable broth)

1 cup mozzarella cheese, shredded

½ cup Parmesan cheese, grated

1 egg, beaten

¼ cup breadcrumbs (optional, for extra binding)

2 tablespoons fresh parsley, finely chopped

1 tablespoon olive oil

¼ teaspoon garlic powder

1 teaspoon dried basil

Directions

Preheat the oven to 375°F (190°C).

In a large bowl, combine the cooked risotto, mozzarella cheese, Parmesan cheese, beaten egg, parsley, garlic powder, and basil.

If the mixture feels too loose, add breadcrumbs, a little at a time, until it sticks together.

Scoop tablespoon-sized portions of the mixture and form them into small, soft balls.

Place on a baking sheet lined with parchment paper.

Lightly drizzle olive oil over the top of each rice ball for extra moisture.

Bake for 12-15 minutes or until the rice balls are golden and set.

Serve warm, optionally with a side of smooth tomato sauce for dipping.

Nutrition Facts (per serving)

200 Calories | 9g Fat | 22g Carbs | 7g Protein

Soft & Creamy Fried Rice

Ingredients

2 tablespoons olive oil

1 cup finely diced carrots

1 small onion, finely chopped

1/2 cup frozen peas

4 cups cooked white rice (softened by adding a little water while reheating)

2 eggs, beaten and scrambled

3 tablespoons low-sodium soy sauce

1 teaspoon toasted sesame oil

1 tablespoon oyster sauce (optional)

Directions

Heat olive oil in a large skillet or non-stick pan over medium heat.

Add the carrots, onion, and peas. Cook for about 5 minutes until softened.

Add the rice, breaking up any clumps. Stir gently, adding a little water if the rice seems too dry.

Push the rice mixture to one side of the pan and scramble the beaten eggs in the empty space. Once scrambled, mix the eggs back into the rice.

Stir in the soy sauce, sesame oil, and optional oyster sauce.

Continue to cook for another 3 minutes until everything is well combined.

Serve immediately.

Nutrition Facts (per serving)

250 Calories | 11g Fat | 29g Carbs | 8g Protein

Potato Pancakes

Ingredients

- 3 cups mashed potatoes
- 2 large eggs
- ½ cup all-purpose flour
- ½ cup shredded cheddar cheese
- 1 teaspoon dried parsley
- salt and pepper to taste, to taste
- vegetable oil, for frying

Directions

1. Preheat a large frying pan or griddle to medium heat.
2. If your potatoes are cold from the fridge, we recommend warming them up slightly and giving them a second mash or beating with an electric mixer so they're easier to work with.
3. In a large bowl add the mashed potatoes, eggs, flour, cheese, parsley, salt, and pepper.
4. Stir the ingredients together.
5. Grease the frying pan/skillet lightly.
6. Form the dough into patties about ¼ cup of batter each. Flatten the patty between your palms.
7. Fry on the one side until golden (about 3-5 minutes), then flip and fry on the second side until golden. Drain on paper towels. Serve with a dollop of sour cream and green onions (optional).

Nutrition Facts (per serving)

Calories 469 | Carbs 25g | Protein 15g | Fat 34g

Herb and Garlic Mashed Potatoes

Ingredients

- 0.17 head garlic, small
- 1 potatoes, medium
- salt to taste
- 8.33ml/0.04 cup whole milk, hot
- 16.67g/0.08 cup unsalted butter
- 0.17-0.33 tbsp parsley
- 0.17-0.33 tbsp dill

Directions

1. Preheat the oven to 200C/400F. Cut the top off the head of garlic to expose the cloves, wrap in aluminum foil and bake for 45-50 minutes until the cloves are very soft. Cool.
2. Boil the peeled and quartered potatoes in salted water until very tender. While the potatoes are cooking, squeeze the garlic cloves out of their peels, they should pop out easily and mash them with a fork in a small bowl. Set aside.

3. Drain the potatoes and steam dry them to get rid of the excess of water. Return them to the pot and add hot milk, start mashing with a potato masher until mostly smooth, then add butter and keep mashing. Start by stirring in 1/2 of the mashed roasted garlic, slowly increase the garlic quantity according to taste, then mash until smooth and most lumps are broken, season with salt to taste. Add the fresh herbs and fold in with a spatula. Serve piping hot with a bit more butter if desired.

Nutrition Facts (per serving)

Calories 255 | Carbs 28g | Protein 6g | Fat: 14g

Soft Corn Tortilla Casserole

Ingredients

12 soft corn tortillas (use soft, pliable tortillas, or soften them by steaming or microwaving)

2 cups shredded rotisserie chicken (finely shredded)

1 cup mild salsa verde (smooth consistency)

1 cup shredded cheddar cheese

1/2 cup sour cream

1 tablespoon olive oil

Directions

Preheat the oven to 350°F (175°C).

Lightly coat a 9x13 baking dish with olive oil.

Tear the corn tortillas into smaller pieces and layer them at the bottom of the baking dish.

In a bowl, combine the shredded chicken and salsa verde, stirring until evenly mixed.

Spread the chicken mixture evenly over the torn tortillas.

Sprinkle the shredded cheese on top.

Cover with foil and bake for 15-20 minutes until bubbly and heated through.

Remove from the oven and top with a dollop of sour cream before serving.

Nutrition Facts (per serving)

310 Calories | 15g Fat | 18g Carbs | 20g Protein

Spaghetti Spaghetti Squash

Ingredients

- 1 Spaghetti Squash
- 1 tablespoon olive oil
- salt and pepper to taste
- 1 pound ground beef
- 1 (14.5 oz) can diced tomatoes
- 1 (15 oz) can tomato paste
- 1 tablespoon italian seasoning (alternatively you could do 1 teaspoon dried oregano and 2 teaspoons dried basil)
- 1/4 teaspoon baking soda

Directions

1. Preheat oven to 400°. Use a fork to puncture the spaghetti squash a lot, like 20 times. Stick it on a plate and microwave it for 3-5 minutes (this makes it easier to cut through). Cut lengthwise in half and remove the seeds and pulp. Coat the inside with a layer of olive oil and cover with a pinch of salt and pepper. Place it cut-side down on a cookie sheet lined with foil and bake at 400° for 40 minutes. Use a fork to scrape the

squash, as it "fluffs" up it turns into beautifully formed noodles.
2. Brown ground beef in a pan over medium-high heat. Drain the fat. Add the tomatoes, tomato sauce, tomato paste, and Italian seasoning. Bring the sauce to a boil and reduce to a simmer for 20 minutes. Add the baking soda and stir thoroughly. Pour sauce over the prepared spaghetti squash noodles.

Nutrition Facts (per serving)

Calories 380 | Carbs 30g | Protein 25g | Fat 18g

Summer Squash Puree

Ingredients

- 2 tablespoons olive oil
- 4 cups sliced summer squash
- 1 ½ cups slice onions
- salt and pepper (to taste)

Directions

1. In a large frying pan, add the oil, squash, and onions.

2. Cook on high heat for ten minutes, stir every one minute. Season with salt and pepper to taste.
3. Added the cooked squash and onions to a blender and blend until a smooth, pureed consistency is reached.

Nutrition Facts (per serving)

Calories 90| Carbs 12g | Protein 2g   Fat 4g

Pink Fluff

Ingredients

- 1 pint cottage cheese
- 1 (3 ounce) box raspberry jello mix
- 1 (20 ounce) can crushed pineapple, drained
- 3 sliced bananas
- 1 (8 ounce) tub frozen whipped topping (like Cool Whip)

Directions

1. In a large mixing bowl, add the cottage cheese and dry jello mix. Mix well.
2. Stir in the pineapple and bananas.

3. Fold in the whipped topping. It is ready to eat right away but it keeps well in the fridge for up to a few days.

Nutrition Facts (8 serving)

Calories 220| Carbs 30g | Protein 10g | Fat 10g

Glazed Carrots

Ingredients

- 6 large carrots, cut lengthwise (could be substituted for a small bag of baby carrots)
- ¼ cup finely chopped pecans
- 1 tablespoon butter
- 3 tablespoons pure maple syrup
- ⅛ teaspoon salt

Directions

1. Take a medium sized saucepan and fill with ½ inch of water. Bring to a boil, add carrots and cover with lid. Cook for 10-12 minutes or until carrots are tender. Drain water and remove carrots.

2. Add butter, maple syrup, and salt to the drained and empty saucepan. While stirring constantly, bring to a boil. Once boiling, reduce heat to a simmer and add carrots. Cook until carrots are glazed and golden brown.
3. Using a blender, food processor, or knife, finely chop pecans. Sprinkle the glazed carrots with the pecans and serve immediately.

Nutrition Facts (per servings)

Calories 120 | Carbs 16g | Protein 1g | Fat 6g

Egg Salad and Avocado

Ingredients

- 2 eggs
- 1 tablespoon mayonnaise
- 1 teaspoon mustard
- 1 ripe avocado

Directions

1. Put eggs in a small pot, cover them with an inch of lukewarm water. Cook on medium heat until it

reaches a rolling boil. Immediately turn off the stove and cover the pot. Let it sit for 10 minutes.
2. Drain the water and fill the pot back up with ice cold water, this stops the eggs from cooking.
3. Peel the eggs and dice them. Stir in the mayonnaise and the mustard.
4. Slice the avocado and take out the pit. Fill each half with egg salad and eat with your favorite spoon.

Nutrition Facts (per serving)

Calories 320 | Fat 24g | Carbohydrates 12g | Protein 14g

5   Chapter Five

SMOOTHIES, SHAKES AND PUREED TREAT RECIPES

Strawberry Rhubarb Smoothie

Ingredients

- 2 cups rhubarb (frozen)
- 2 cups strawberries (frozen)
- 3 cups orange juice
- 3 tbsp honey

Directions

1. Add all ingredients to your best blender and blend until smooth. Feel free to add more orange juice if you would like a more liquid consistency for your smoothie.

Nutrition Facts (per serving)

Calories 160| Carbs 38g | Protein 2g | Fat 1g

Strawberry Lemonade Smoothie

Ingredients

- 1½ cups lemonade
- 1½ cups frozen strawberries
- ¾ cup frozen peaches
- 1 cup lime sherbet

Directions

1. Combine all ingredients into your favorite blender and blend to a smooth consistency.

Nutrition Facts (per serving)

Calories 180| Carbs 38g | Protein 2g | Fat 2g

Summer Smoothie

Ingredients

- 1 ½ cups mango passion fruit juice

- ¾ cup frozen peaches
- 1 ½ cups frozen strawberries
- 1 cup orange sherbet

Directions

1. Combine all Ingredients in your most powerful blender. Blend to a smooth, drinkable consistency.

Nutrition Facts (per serving)

Calories 190| Carbs 42g | Protein 1g | Fat 2g

Zucchini Smoothie

Ingredients

- 2 cups chopped zucchini
- 1 cup frozen mango
- 1 cup pineapple chunks with the juice
- ½ cup coconut milk
- 1 teaspoon lime juice

Directions

1. Combine all ingredients in your favorite blender and blend until smooth.

Nutrition Facts (per serving)

Calories 140| Carbs 24g | Protein 2g | Fat 7g

Almond Milk

Ingredients

- 1 cup almonds
- 4 cups water
- 1 pinch salt
- 2 dates (this is optional, it will make the almond milk sweeter, you could also sweeten it with agave syrup)

Directions

1. In a bowl, cover the almonds in water. Let the almonds soak for 8 hours.
2. Drain the water from the bowl. Transfer the almonds to a blender and add 4 cups of water with

a pinch of salt. You could also add 2 dates for extra sweetness. Blend until smooth.
3. Line a pitcher with a nut milk bag, pour the blended liquid into the nut milk bag. Twist and squeeze the nut milk bag, expressing as much liquid as you can into the pitcher. Drink right away or store in the fridge for up to a few days.

Nutrition Facts (per serving)

Calories 60 | Carbs 4g | Protein 1g | Fat 2.5g

Chocolate Cherry Banana Smoothie

Ingredients

- 1 cup almond milk (normal milk can be used, but almond milk tastes better for this recipe)
- ½ cup fresh spinach (packed densely into the measuring cup)
- 1 tablespoon cocoa powder
- 1 frozen banana
- 1 cup frozen cherries
- ¼ cup almonds

Directions

1. Add all ingredients to your most trusted blender and blend until desired consistency is reached.

Nutrition Facts (per serving)

Calories 320| Carbs 50g | Protein 6g | Fat 12g

Blueberry Banana Smoothie

Ingredients

- 1 (20 ounce) can pineapple chunks
- 1 frozen banana
- 2 cups frozen blueberries

Directions

1. Put all ingredients into a blender and blend until it reaches the desired consistency.

Nutrition Facts (per serving)

Calories 180| Carbs 44g | Protein 2g | Fat 1g

Almond Pear Milkshake

Ingredients

- 1 cup vanilla ice cream
- 1 (15 ounce) can pears, drained
- ¼ cup almonds
- ¼ teaspoon cinnamon

Directions

1. Combine all ingredients in a powerful blender and blend until smooth. You could add a little extra ice cream if you would like it thicker.

Nutrition Facts (per serving)

Calories 340 | Carbs 40g | Protein 5g | Fat 18g

Mango Pear Smoothie

Ingredients

- 1 (15 ounce) can pears (don't drain it)
- 1 empty pear can full of frozen mangoes

Directions

1. Pour the canned pears (with the liquid) into a blender. Use the empty can as your measuring cup. Fill it up with frozen mangoes and add that to the blender too. Blend until smooth.

Nutrition Facts (per serving)

Calories 220| Carbs 55g | Protein 1g | Fat 0g

Blueberry Peach Smoothie

Ingredients

- 1 (15 ounce) can peaches
- 1 empty peach can full of frozen blueberries

Directions

1. Pour the can of peaches (with all the syrup) in a blender. Fill the empty can up with frozen blueberries and put that in the blender too. Blend until smooth.

Nutrition Facts (per serving)

Calories 180| Carbs 45g | Protein 2g | Fat 0g

Mango-Raspberry-Pineapple Smoothie

Ingredients

- 1 cup frozen mangoes
- 1 cup frozen raspberries
- 1 (20 ounce) can pineapple chunks

Directions

1. Combine the mangoes, raspberries, and the pineapple chunks (with the juice) and blend in a blender until the desired consistency is reached.

Nutrition Facts (per serving)

Calories 240| Carbs 60g | Protein 2g | Fat 1g

The Banana Milkshake

Ingredients

- 2 peeled ripe bananas
- 1½ cup vanilla ice cream
- ½ cup milk
- ½ teaspoon cinnamon

Directions

1. Place all ingredients in your favorite blender and blend until smooth. I think it's best eaten right away.

Nutrition Facts (per serving)

Calories 380 | Carbs 50g | Protein 8g | Fat 18g

Carrot Cake Smoothie Bowl

Ingredients

- ½ cup cooked carrots

- 1 banana
- ½ cup Greek yogurt
- ½ teaspoon cinnamon
- 1 teaspoon maple syrup
- Optional: ground walnuts for garnish

Directions

1. Add all ingredients to a blender.
2. Blend until smooth and creamy.
3. Pour into a bowl, sprinkle ground walnuts if desired, and serve.

Nutrition Facts (per serving)

Calories 200 | Fat 0g | Carbs 36g | Protein 7g

Printed in Dunstable, United Kingdom